WINDS
OF
SILENCE

WINDS
OF
SILENCE

RASO

MISTY RIDGE PRESS
MISSOULA, MONTANA

ISBN: 979-8-9851843-0-3
Cover and interior design by Open Heart Designs

To all drawn toward the One,
and its inexpressible music of silence.

CONTENTS

RETURNING, SHE BEGINS

The poems of this collection are songs of a person on the Path. They are expressions of a journey, its flowers, clear reflections, dense fogs, shifting winds, opening broad vistas. I hope the glimpses offered here find a resonance with your life and pathways.

"Move around your center, go on moving inwards, and a moment comes when every movement stops. Then there is no sound: you have entered silence. This silence is divine, this silence is bliss, this silence is the purpose of all life...."
—*Osho*

BOUNDARIES ARE FEATHERS

RIPPLES

standing
where all melts into emptiness
on that firmness
yet oh the ripples
shining gold and indigo
spreading on the surface
of the stream

BOUNDARIES ARE FEATHERS

Boundaries are feathers,
feathering the space
between the part and the whole.
The feathers flutter.
The whole flows
on its unfathomable journey.
Something akin to bliss, but it is silent.
A deep broad valley.
A canyon where a cold silent river
slips through ancient stone.

CENTER THE LONGING

Smoke from the chimney pours into the yard,
churning, tumbling, turning the air thick and fragrant
with the return of trees,
the burning bodies of trees rising as smoke
and plunging with the roiling wind
low across the ground

Center the longing
on the column of the spine

Pain is an interpretation,
a boundary condensed around something wild,
and the wind of the soul
and the wind of the wild heart of existence
waving its branches
releasing secrets evanescent as air
long to mingle
to pour together through the unknown
as one

FORM IS TOO SMALL

form is too small
it constricts
holds to that which breaks
cleaves to hope and sorrow

       waving
       gliding
       moving between worlds
       holding nothing

HAWK'S DIVE

Frightened flock of birds arising out of meadow grass
So I lift out of myself, fluttering in my chest
and look outward to choose

Inward
Plummeting in a hawk's dive toward an unseen target
Falling headlong, let the small birds rise in alarm
They will settle again on small perches, or near the
    quiet stream
Peck again at insects in the long grass or scoop them
    from the air above shining water

Let the hawk dive

A CIRCLE OF SMALL HILLS

the person stutters
clutching at identifiers
locators
localizers
to give her a form and place
a smaller place
that might provide
a defining circle
a place of coziness and blessed interference
a circle of small hills
confining the expanse
so the sky does not fray away
so far

oh it frays her
it swirls through her flesh
as the heart of delicacy
and the dreams
the human dreams
fray in the unseen wind

Venturing forth

LEAVING THE BRIGHTLY LIT PLACE

leaving the brightly lit place to
extraordinary magic
diffused deep
gray misty
still hovers
known unknown

soughing day is a cloak in which
I am a fold, a thread, a feeling
nakedly wriggling in a dream sea
fearless who dares not
meadow-stepper
sleep-craver
face up to a
fine rainy
streaked sky
pale dawn

FULL MOON AND FOG

full moon and fog cresting the mountains
pine trees and scented brush
loosened again
the earth breathes through me

the womb of the mysterious has opened
vastness drops away
my consciousness
plummets
the fall is so great
the exhilaration passes
the dizziness passes
the nausea, the longing passes
the stone in the soul passes
and a great ache flowers
deep bottomless space
the ache of the ephemeral
ache of dissolving form
ache of moonlight that passes
coolness rising
rippling across the senses
not remaining

when the soul is moving but not by events,
thoughts, actions, prescriptions, categories of time
moving from a vague origin toward
what once was a destination
by means of an ill-defined and sluggish cyclone

circular motion
undulation
the rolling of the ground
pitches my equilibrium from me
I crouch low and shuffle
towards a glimmer of a path

try not to let my raw jealous fear
tip to the angle of pouring and escape
images are dusky and fluid yet
as I am
I am here
at the root
the root of purification

root here
root
in purification

WAVES

all my wounds are surface scratches
they cut only the armor of my soul
they crash with a wave on yellow sand
and quietly expire with the foam

how little the troubles that torment me touch me
in sweeping water even small scars are healed
I am left with only the long trailing backsides
of waves, then mysteriously
they too are gone

RAINY NIGHT COMFORT

spray of rain
flung by the wind upon my window
the swelling rustle of pear leaves

IT ISN'T COMPANY I SEEK

It isn't company I seek but shelter
arms, human warmth
not shelter perhaps but sharing
not events but this that fills me now
emptiness
facelessness
I do not stretch so far
I need to feel you
our commonness
warmth without boundary
I am lost without boundaries
and need more than just myself alone
thinning and dissolving endlessly
but to reverberate
let go in you

to meet so simply is rare
I do not want to become recognizable
I do not want to retreat
I want to be held
do not comfort me
drown with me
into me
hold me

AT THE CENTER

at the center
the only solidity
has no substance

the only place on which to stand
is bottomless

the only place of orientation
is the unending opening
of empty space

in all directions
indefinable
tide of tenderness
softness beyond bearing
can such innocence survive?

FEARING AND FLAMING

fearing and flaming
within the heart of the fire
orange heart
heart of existence

from the back
knowing is from the back
like the flame around a log
curves from underneath
unless I can sink into the
back, the underside,
that which is behind,
I stay locked out
I cannot move outside
a tiny boundary
skin, and the binding of mind

slipping out, as if melted, pooling
as namelessness, shoreless,
spreading across a landscape
reflecting stars, no ripple

A SINGLE POINT

searching only
a single point
to reckon by
what blooms is
the seed of
the flowering
of emptiness

a heart cannot hold it
it will break
I am breaking

IN THE PRESENCE

Something happens.
Like a fizzy drink, tiny bubbles rising.
Like sitting behind a waterfall except
it's falling up.
A bright indistinguishable panorama
rolling slowly upward
like a curtain rising and rising
and rising
with the same kind of expectation
as when some magnificent spectacle
is about to begin
and you are small
and all is velvet and
glittering chandeliers
except it is taking off like
a great bright balloon broken free
of its moorings
and instead of miniature dancers
on a stage far below
you are looking
up, up, up
into endless sky.

THE ONE CHOICE

REAL CRYING

when *real* crying happens
there is no stopping it

the heaving of a sea within
a wave swelling
the wave doesn't even notice
the dock pilings snapping
doesn't see the pier break loose
from its shore moorings
in that way, the constraints
around the heart
flatten outward at the swell of tears
the chest breaks apart
the sea wall crumbles

as this wave approaches
it is better to yield
let it flood through beaches, streets, gardens
let it scour the landscape into
something unrecognizable

NO APOLOGIES

I'm going to miss if I can't get inside
I can chase after it full bore, tripping,
    being angry, then excited, then exhilarated,
    then in the dumps, then feeling proud, then
    crawling like a worm
Or I can choose to be inside
Lighter, with nowhere to go
Nowhere to go!
Then, if I am aflame it is the exquisite beauty of flaming
No destination
Then, if I am weeping it is existence weeping
No comparison, no need
Then, totality opens and opens
    and opens and opens
    not proving anything
    not demonstrating anything
Then, my own feet are on the earth
No apologies

TIDAL JOURNEY

on a wave of laughter
I ride out the top of my head
in a small boat
unnoticed

a vast sea surrounds me with no horizon
there is no tilting plane of water to catch a sun's fire
no division even up and down
but the sea's substance is more like
foam, or sea spray, and I sail weightless,
windless, substanceless, indistinguishable
in a gentle blaze of twilight, open-eyed

until the re-forming tide pulls at my butterfly boat
and a body wavers in the reversing current
eyes just glimpse a sublime intimation
as I am flung bone and sinew on this familiar shore
tangled in strands of hopeless hilarity
the face catches, and closes

BEYOND CAPTURE IN ANY DIMENSION

She pulls on the threads
gathering them toward a skein
to form them into a pleasing coil
that would relieve the heart of
its vertigo
its fretting in-between

Today the threads pull back,
resist the weaving of pattern,
tugging toward their disparate origins
in the indivisible One

Can she follow even a single strand
to the knowing in its dissolving root
with the tide receding in all directions?

Can hovering also be a Way,
nothing known or followed
at all?

THE DOWN-PULLER

the down-puller
is crotchety
testy
her picture would
look hunched
squat
her eyes dart about
finding proof
that understanding is
nil
power tripping
great
unconsciousness
swallows the light
she must
be shrewd
defend the flame
battle the power of
darkness
sneaking within
cresting without
the down-puller
worships the
great deity No
guardian of
safety
guiding light of
definition

HEART VIBRATING LIKE A DRUM

heart vibrating like a drum
falling back
not the small sorrow
not caught in the small sorrow
but the current of the great stream,
the great current sweeping past my body,
the brush of an autumn leaf, drowned,
scoring my skin for a moment and gone

yes, now, craving comfort,
or falling into a well of love,
yes but that too is not
the great stream, the stream of dissolution,
an unending current,
and nowhere, no destination,
no reason for this moment, or to pursue
significance in this moment,
or to grieve in this moment.

Aiyeee.
Dry leaves.
Plunging into the dry autumn leaves of the heart.

THE POET LOST HIS WAY

"My life has been the poem I would have writ,
But I could not both live and utter it."
— Henry David Thoreau

Billowing clouds of ice crystals
scud across crusted snow
loosed by a wild wending wind
from laden branches
now wildly waving

Sky clouds too shape and reshape nimbly
pouring west to east, south to north
sun emerging from days of pale and gray
to catch the glint of crystal
reveal shades and qualities of green and
gold and tawny indistinguishable
on dimmer days

Oh it hurts to read their cold
and heady analyses, dissecting your pain
as if pain defined your life
Not knowing, not grasping, inexperienced
in encompassing SILENCE, and
her benificence, her bestowing of
wisdom no pen can popularize,
no theory can explain.
So your life can be boxed, and appreciated
in its category, and we can admire
and praise your turn of a phrase, your
hard-hitting eloquence, incisive commentary
and trivialize your battles
into psychological diagnoses.

I have been trying on your anger,
your bitter judgments and cultural myopia.
Anger echoes in me — oh yes —
when I surface to the hard-edged world
and bitterly regard blind arrogance
claiming the globe entire — and now the
stars — for war, for greed, for dominance.
And I search for what might be my myopia
declaimed through veils I cannot see.

Our compulsion to define, explain, reduce.

Without touching SILENCE
nothing will be understood
and the hullaballoo of your brilliant mind
battling with demons within and without
will seem the thing itself and not
a path to the quenching of thirst,
howsoever sipped, in the desert.

"the poet lost his way in later years,
literary output never again achieved"

no guide except Nature and few old books
thorniness or judgment turning away friends
your own terrible hungers nipping at your heels
hearing the call — the deeper call —
of that which transcends.

HIDDEN LIFE

I dive
into a nonhuman land
unjustifyable
and without utility
unraveled

the pattern I was raised to share
that binds our worlds
into recognizable shapes
and segments of time

stands apart and closed in
upon its circle of warmth
a circle of warmth
howsoever predictable
interwoven contracts and longings
future plans and present exchanges

I too have longings
quieting them
hush now
listen
in gentle evening light
the hidden life may be revealed

bright yellow arnica spilling over a low stump
warm bark of fir and pine through spring's intense greenery
hush now, listen
evensong begins

LIKE A SACRIFICE

like a
sacrifice

made sacred

the creation
has claimed
my limbs
my blood
it has dissolved
my bones
it convulses
as me
what once was me
turning
flooding
swallowing
condensing
to the spiral of origin
infintesimal
immense
alight

DISEMBODIMENT

The ecstacy of embodiment is in
DISEMBODIMENT
Ecstasy is the loss of form
I join with
the movement of the whole
I participate with
DE-CREATION
My body becomes
      a shifting pattern
            of all bodies
Liquid
Light

THE ONE CHOICE

14 degrees below zero at night
barely creeping above zero by day

gray sky tones the forest
to dark green and burnt sienna
snow unlit and pale holds to fronds of fir

is there remembrance?

despite the challenges
which are ALWAYS available
the choices of each moment

the choice of each moment
superceding the choices
that harden into choosing
and then protecting
from the clamoring of other choices

and yet if there
is no choosing
the clamoring picking apart
the flesh of the life like
coyotes at a carcass
where nothing remains but
a few chewed bones
the CHOICE too dragged into the
bushes and devoured to become
someone else's scat on a game path
somewhere

but the one choice
so stark
so indefensible
when the back frays
into the existence itself
the heart falls open so wide
that every other choice
and every footpath
into the particularity
of choosing
is swallowed in
a dissolving tide
of emptiness

SIERRA SPINE

will you be my bones
deeper than bones
to the root of skeleton
to the vibrating imprint of
structure coming into being
becoming bones
the root becoming the core
from which all flows

will you be my core
elemental, revealed
will you reside as my core
from which beauty may flow
and dance and color
yielding to that which is

held and yielded up
by each and every being
fleck of stone
browning needle of pine
green beings
gust of wind on water

will you be my bones
bones of this life

SEASON OF HEAT

"Historical data is not the midline of our experience."
—Emilie Conrad

The lilacs, still fragrant, have whitened.
Crimson maple has taken on its summer plumage of burgundy
   and rust.
Intense green edges beyond plumpness toward a season of heat.
Small puffs of cloud rise through the western trees,
drift slowly across an expanse of blue.
I sit in the shade of a furrowed and lichen-bedecked ponderosa,
the meadow beyond still green and waving
with fruiting grasses, spangled swaths of yellow asters.

Clouds rise from the unseen, drifting, so slowly.
Touches a yearning.
Chest wants to expand and expand....
heart wants to break... open...
melt into another human animal, another body warm
with sun and sweat and longing.

The yearning. Touches loins. Throat a deep cavern.
Touches feathers of memory.
Those rare times when it seemed it would be fulfilled.
Rare moments—
naked in the sun on hot granite by a lake of clear azure,
or held encircled in warmth atop a coastal knoll
breathing the special musk of redwood forest and
gazing toward the sea, in a city park with all love flowing
entangled in burgundy on the grass, or on a hot spring slope
up Mill Creek, crushing the fragrant foliage with our bodies—
It seemed it would be fulfilled.
The yearning.
The immolation in love.

Summer clouds, slowly shaping and re-shaping.

The illusion of yearning is in its eccentricity.
It chases after phantasmagoria, hopes blindly for union.
"Can I abandon myself to life, to thee?"
Edges into dream, carries baggage. Falls apart, again.

So, dissolve then.
Let the heart break.
Dissolve, then.
The whole makes love to the whole, right here.

THE JOURNEY

just when I seem to have
turned to stone
or dead wood
the journey opens again

the un-way

the way here, where
there is no arrival

ripping through the body
the power of the rose
the power of delicacy
weaving impossibly fine
tendrils of light into
dark retreated corners
the power of blooming
which recognizes no enemy
the power of love
which cannot participate
in ancient warring
but rises through locked and armed places
revealing the fortress
to be a garden

THE BALANCE RETAINS ITSELF

WAITING

waiting
as the holy of holies
no business
only allowing these magnificent circles to keep rising and
arcing, through thighs, through the open landscape
of my chest, like several suns rising
comets streaming a fine trail of red and gold
obliterating the addiction to the mundane
the habit of looking first at the map
circling duties and tasks on a projected route
girding the luxurious body into an armor as habitual as
the morning news, as preparing to march
across a two-dimensional landscape and survive

oh beauty
rising suns crisscrossing gold and purple
filling cavities already twitching toward necessity
with a watercolor wash that leaves the body bodiless
beauty that does not care to read the warnings
cannot be convinced there is a higher value
waiting
that's all
to give you back your reign

SOUND

sound
never formulating
remaining pure
penetrating into each part
as pure vibration

the flower begins to open
around the sound

without preconceiving
it becomes vast

my arms are the arms
of existence
relaxing they trail
in unfathomable waters
the fire kindled within
consumes all boundaries
consumes the flower
ignites the ocean to flames

never consumed
coolness rests

ECSTASY ITSELF

ecstasy itself
is the release of constraint

the opening
the spreading
the tingling in the flesh
when that which is held
the clenched
becomes a kind of painful tearing stretch
except the pain transmutates
the binding comes apart
into a web of gossamer strands
vibrating as light

ecstasy itself
is the release of constraint

hovering as fraying light
where beyond
lies nothing
no experience
no bliss

IT MUST FLOW THROUGH

It must flow through
Emerging and returning together
Like a hollow bamboo
Like a river course
Like a rock in the river holds its place
dissolving as it stands

How broad it is
when unrestrained
The volume can be immense

The balance retains itself
Behind the eyes
there need be nobody

Only the balance
with all its potentialities

but it must flow through

LIKE A TIDE IT RETURNS

the sound of wind rises and falls
trees become waves of tossing branches
against a cloud-pale sky in the warming sunshine
cold spring morning
green gold waves

the heart flows out, lifts into the dance
yearning and a hungry exhilaration draw it
far across the waving landscape
to where, on beach unseen, it
breaks into foaming crescents of thought
soaks into sands
no longer of this day

the blessed moon below the horizon
or the gravitational pull of a greater longing
or the shadow of deep remembrance
or the master's grace
pulls on the myriad frayings of mind

like a tide it returns
flowing back with that inexorable inescapability
here again
where in empty open gratitude
the sound of wind rises and falls

MOONSCAPE

gently removing
the sticky tentacles
of *desire*

bleakness and disorientation
are the moonscape
between
the populated world
of dream and doing
and the wordless world
where reality sings

endure it
do the work
let *go*

THE GATE

In my lower back: a gate.
So simple that rather than entering
I take off in search of something
more colorful and ornate.

Once more: the gate.
The gravitational pull so subtle,
in an instant I am off again
in restless search.

Or, allowing the pull:
Solidity wavers to nearly transparent,
an exquisite unraveling of what in a dream defined me
I am only a density, and as the gate pulls,
the density thins.

Here is the entrance. If I enter,
words cease, I cease, no one returns.
I stand at the edge in fascination,
blurring in a high airless wind.

Yet I formulate. I seek formulation.
Only the sensation of
the imminence of dissolution.
I retain myself.

Great gate! I am afraid even to ask:
pull me into the brilliance of the abyss.

THE AMBROSIAL HOUR
The nectar-filled time of dawn and dusk

We are always at the interface.
Always standing at the gateless gate,
where form flows into the formless
and the formless flows into form.
It is.
It is the isness.

That is the back.
The back streams with eternity.
It billows from nothingness,
contiguous with nothingness,
   yet shaping
   yet billowing.

The front condenses into shapes
   with their surfaces
   that appear to divide.
Yet the planes of the river's currents
   which slide past each other
   in myriad vortices
The streaming of wind across my face,
   its hand dividing into numberless
   fingers which delicately curl through
   a strand of hair,
   across a lip
   or spin a single pine needle through sunlight
Are also formless.

Form is formless.
Giving birth to both.
Residing in both.
Streaming with both
in the ambrosial hour.

AT THE EDGE

the ache at the edge
of silence

mouth and throat swollen with
the buds of words

heart cracked poised above
that chasm
from which
when it falls
if it falls

only boiling vapors arise
unaddressed

IN THE SHADE OF STONE

Sitting in the shade of stone,
a huge glacial erratic in a rounded cube
festooned with lichen in green and gold circles
a layer of quartz covering its top,
weathering here in delicate sheets,
crumbling into brightly flecked gravel
or thin brittle shells which will weather
to gravel and sand and mix with relinquished
plant bodies to form soil

Sitting in this square of shade,
sun edging around to face me,
the lake glistening and lapping,
rippling in indigo and olive, turquoise
becoming blue purple amber in the shallows
before running up on stony shore
and an edge of tufted grass and sedge,
lapping here, a few bubbles floating,
silently pulsing back across the lake
where sunlight sparkles

Sitting quietly, sipping from a red enamel cup,
watching lacy cloud shadows slip down
snowfields across the canyon
on the vertical faces of a massive divide

The hikers didn't see me as they picked their way
across rock and snow, tromping steadily
with the clicking of their trekking poles

They didn't glance back, but skirted
the lake and dropped out of sight

Would they have noticed me, had they turned?

Closer to stone now.
Closer to the dry tufts of grass
that wave stiffly in the wind.
Closer to the small purple trumpets,
the ripples that peak into
a glint of sunlight,
shift from olive to purple,
return to lake.

AIKI NO KURAI
The secret of Aiki

approaching... something...
a place to stand
but there is nothing
'how can a snowflake exist in a raging fire?'

she pulls away
and returns to wrestling with images,
dispersing thoughts

then again this delicate dangling
of being into
undifferentiated being

could I touch from here?
standing on this trailing nothingness
would agency open—*aiki no kurai?*

the barest of acknowledgements
this *is* the place to stand
the only firmness
but the capacity is small
the least wind brings back
two... many... myriad...

deepen capacity
risk all
to dissolve into one

ALL OF NATURE IS AT REST

at rest
it is unified
all of nature is at rest

the weight of my hand
resting on stone
or cool soil
or wet moss
or the ragged soaked cone of a fir
or the still-green leaves of tiny violet
cupped to hold a drop of rainwater
or a brown leaf melting, its edges dark
clump of young grass like spider silk

our doorways open
it is communion
not two

and then we are supported from
everywhere
informed from all corners
by waves, and the fractals of waves

chasing, it closes
it is the nature of things
no blame, just a law
from before existence, preceding existence

if we choose to isolate ourselves
in dreams and fears and hopes and desires
the flow of blessed information
the delicate latticework of support
does not invade the boundary we hold

WHAT DID NORMAN CLYDE FEEL*

What did Norman Clyde feel
waking of a morning here
stone jutting into another cerulean sky
knobbed granite strewn with glacial erratics
green and purple ripples across turquoise water
seeding grasses bobbing
a clump of shooting stars mostly gone
willow just releasing cottony tufts
and waving gracefully in its characteristic stiff way
as the season barely turns toward autumn

did he ever feel he had seen it all
sated his senses
known his beloved
these mountains and waters
scalloped prostrate clusters of whitebark pine
heather mats

had he melted? did he weep?
with the beauty and its
uncompromising revelation
life and death, love and impassivity
as one forever and enduring

had his bones turned to feldspar and quartzite
one day slipping into another
as a symphony of moon, star and sun, waxing
and waning in a rhythm known wordless by the blood

did he have his grouchy days
when eyes were shuttered by human needs
out of sorts, irritable,
pained to have lost the naked truth
that had filled and dissolved him
had seemed
this time
to be permanent
a transmutation
the fulfillment of this
elemental hunger

was he tired when he shouldered his
90 pound pack with its Virgil and Homer and
poems not yet complete
did he say—this time I'll find myself
a little house
a woman
I'll teach in the high school
I'll guide those who want to climb
the peaks where I stood alone
and silent
in the immensity

was he proud when he emerged
from his wild wanderings
into town
to be the one, the legendary,

needing to preserve and enhance
his one claim, his one fame,
to be that maverick mountaineer
who read classics by firelight
and scrambled up impossible peaks
and needed no one
no human company
no one
but these mountains
their fragrances
their wind, their storms

was he lonely
did he dream of a different life
was he too much a curmudgeon
too strange and restless for convivial ways

or did he hold the heart of this place
his own heart broken open
did he walk alight

*Renowned and enigmatic mountaineer Norman Clyde (1885-1972)
spent much of his life alone in the High Sierra.*

SILENCE

silence
a word until
it descends
and is wordless

pale clouds burgeoning
through the pale sky of sunset
outlined by an edge of fire
evening of a hot day
texture of the road
texture of pavement
it opens
silence

now evening darkens
a bat flits through the yard's open sky
mama turkey moves silently with her remaining
    half-grown brood of three
they skirt the forest and disappear up the hill

pale clouds drift
through the pale sky of dusk
they metamorphose to charcoal
fragrance of earth rises, mixes with pine bark
august evensong is a chorus of chirping
they're still here
here
dissolving into
silence

Returning, she begins

RETURNING, SHE BEGINS

Witnessing
The hard-edged thought-form
is absorbed
Witnessing
there is no time even for recognition
Before identification
there is a shimmering
a bare glimpse of an apparition
that disappears into
patterns of light
that cascade and swirl
in an arising tide of awe
Witnessing
the oceanic display
the bursting heart
is absorbed
Witnessing
even hallelujah
is burnt in the fire

SO MUCH MORE

I would like to give you so much more, he said.
But I cannot give that for which you are not ready.
It could be detrimental to your growth,
perhaps for lives.

But he gave — he overflowed —
he flooded me with love, washed away wounds,
broke my heart again and again,
opened crusted pathways to perception,
seeing, insight.

You have to be courageous.
You have to risk.
You have to risk all.

I would like to survive!

It is a different risk.
The risk of one's own being.
The risk of all structure
that divides and codifies.
The risk to perceive without a perceiver.
Knowing, deeply knowing, because of your grace,
that there is no true perception until the perceiver
is gone, emptied of the the self.

DHARMA

simply remembering to observe the vessel
it overflows, beauteous, restful
seven suns alight

ACKNOWLEDGMENTS

My heartfelt appreciation goes to Jamie Tipton of Open Heart Designs for her artistry, friendship and exquisite sense of design. A deep bow to the teachers who have illuminated the Path and given encouragement and inspiration to continue, even when the way has been fearful and tangled. Thank you to the beloved companions of the Way. Unending gratitude flows to the mystic Osho.

Raso grew up on the western edge of the North American continent where ocean tides, ancient forest and high alpine wilderness became her lifetime teachers. From an early age she was drawn to an ecstatic and expressive path, which was tempered and enhanced by the disciplines of Aikido and a committed path of meditation. Her other works include *Iridescent Wings*, a companion volume of poetry; *Alaya, Songs for Earth and Sky*, an offering of music; and *Voice*, a multimedia play exploring effects of the McCarthy era in the United States from a child's perspective. Raso lives in western Montana, where she tends with her partner an area of forested land, teaches Aikido, plays music and continues walking the pathless path of meditation and love.

www.ingramcontent.com/pod-product-compliance
Lightning Source LLC
Chambersburg PA
CBHW051548120626
46551CB00013B/1416